There are three types of gorillas in Africa. All gorillas are very similar to each other in many ways, so most scientists say that all gorillas belong to a single group, or *species*. But there are some important differences between gorillas that come from different parts of Africa—so the scientists have divided gorillas into three regional types, or *subspecies*. These are called the Western Lowland gorilla, the Eastern Lowland gorilla, and the Mountain gorilla.

As you might guess from these names, some gorillas live at lower altitudes (Lowland), while others live at higher altitudes (Mountain). But no matter what the altitude is, *all* gorillas live in very similar kinds of places—in dense forests, where there are a lot of different kinds of plants. This is because gorillas are very large animals, and they must have huge amounts of plant food to eat every day.

In the past, all three gorilla subspecies had much larger areas to live in than they have today. In fact, their ranges may have been more than *twice* as large. But recently, the weather in some parts of Africa has grown drier, and the forests have grown smaller as a result. And people have started to cut down the great forests, to make room for farms and to harvest the timber. With every passing day, there seems to be less room in Africa for the magnificent gorillas.

Eastern Lowland gorillas live in rain forests of central Africa. Their range is located more than 600 miles east of the Western Lowland gorilla range. In general, Eastern gorillas are a bit larger than their western cousins and darker in color. There are probably only about 5,000 of these animals living in the wild today, and they can only be seen at a few zoos.

EASTERN LOWLAND GORILLA
Gorilla gorilla graueri

WESTERN LOWLAND GORILLA
Gorilla gorilla gorilla

Almost all gorillas in zoos are Western Lowland gorillas. These beautiful animals come from tropical forests of west Africa. They are the smallest of the gorilla subspecies, but still very large. A fully grown male may weigh more than 400 pounds (181 kilograms). There is a great deal of variation in the hair color on these animals—from black to grayish-brown. And the hair is usually shorter than other gorilla subspecies. The range of Western gorillas is huge (as you can see on the map). But there are probably no more than 35,000 gorillas living in it.

Both kinds of lowland gorillas are very similar to each other. But Mountain gorillas are different from the others in many ways. It is easy to see some of these differences when you compare a male lowland gorilla (at left) with a male Mountain gorilla (below).

The heads of male Mountain gorillas are higher and more pointed. And their noses have a wider gap in the middle. Lowland males often have a reddish patch of hair on their heads, but Mountain males do not.

☐ WESTERN LOWLAND GORILLAS

☐ EASTERN LOWLAND GORILLAS

■ MOUNTAIN GORILLAS

Mountain gorillas are the largest of all gorillas. Fully grown males may weigh more than 500 pounds (227 kilograms). The hair on these gorillas is often very long and very black. This is because the animals live high up in the mountains, where it sometimes gets cold. The dark, thick hair absorbs heat from the sun better and keeps the body heat from escaping. Mountain gorillas are the rarest of all gorillas. There are fewer than 500 of them in the wild, and none in zoos.

MOUNTAIN GORILLA
Gorilla gorilla beringei

Gorillas look like people

in many ways. For example, they have two arms and two legs, with hands and feet that look similar to ours. And a gorilla's head and body are similar in many ways to a human head and body.

But there are many differences as well. For instance, a gorilla's feet can be used to grab things. And the brain in a gorilla's head is not as big as a human brain. On these pages, you'll find other similarities and differences.

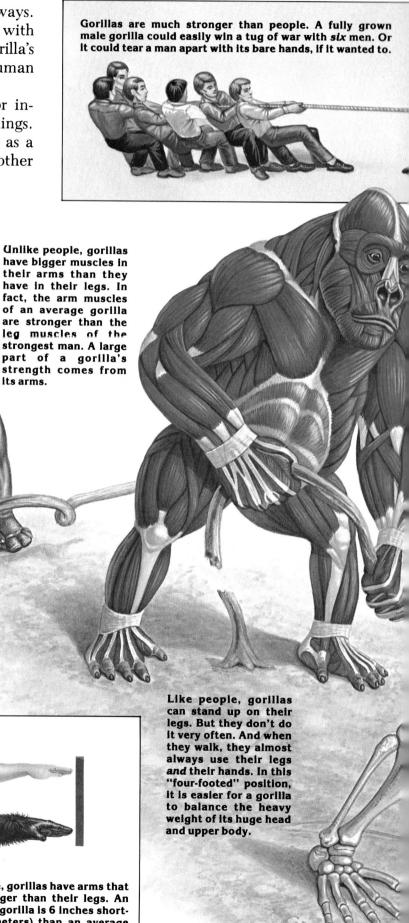

Gorillas are much stronger than people. A fully grown male gorilla could easily win a tug of war with *six* men. Or it could tear a man apart with its bare hands, if it wanted to.

Unlike people, gorillas have bigger muscles in their arms than they have in their legs. In fact, the arm muscles of an average gorilla are stronger than the leg muscles of the strongest man. A large part of a gorilla's strength comes from its arms.

Under a gorilla's dark hair, the skin is also dark. Sometimes, baby gorillas are born with patches of pinkish skin —but it gets darker as they grow older.

Like people, gorillas can stand up on their legs. But they don't do it very often. And when they walk, they almost always use their legs *and* their hands. In this "four-footed" position, it is easier for a gorilla to balance the heavy weight of its huge head and upper body.

Unlike people, gorillas have arms that are much longer than their legs. An average male gorilla is 6 inches shorter (15 centimeters) than an average man. But the gorilla's arms are about *one foot longer* (30 centimeters).

The faces of gorillas are different from each other, in the same way that human faces are all different. In fact, the best way to tell one gorilla from another is to look at their faces. Which one of these gorillas looks most intelligent? Which one seems angry? And which one appears to be thinking about something?

Most of a gorilla's bones and muscles are very similar to yours. But the shape of the gorilla's body is different. For one thing, the stomach is much larger than the chest. This is because gorillas eat very bulky food, and they need lots of room to hold all of it.

The hands of gorillas are very similar to human hands in a number of ways. They have five fingers, with a thumb that can be used for grabbing things. They have fingernails instead of claws. And they have fingerprints that look like human prints. Can you see some ways in which gorilla hands are *different* from human hands?

When a gorilla walks, it uses the backs of its fingers like a foot. This is called *knuckle walking*. Gorillas and chimpanzees are the only animals that walk this way.

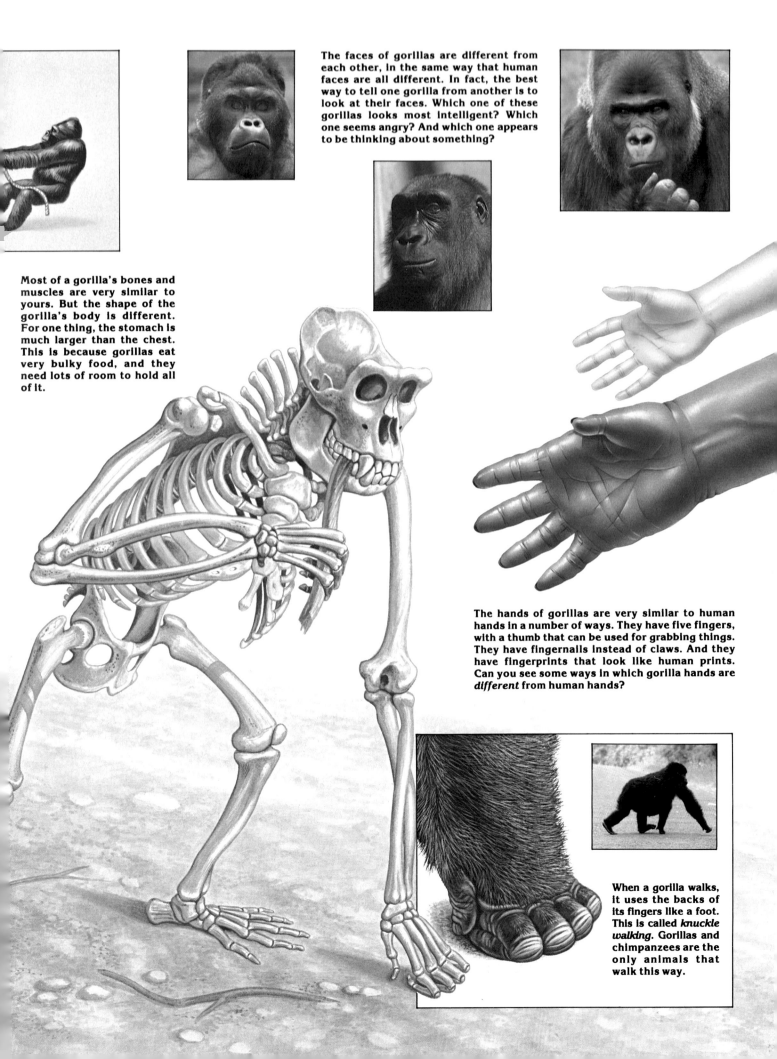

The family is the main social unit of gorillas. All gorillas live in family groups called *troops*, and these range in size from five to thirty gorillas.

The head of each family is an adult male gorilla called a *silverback*. As a male grows older and stronger, the hair on his back slowly turns gray. By the time he has grown old enough to take command of a family, a male's back may be almost totally gray—and this is where we get the name "silver back."

Life in a gorilla family is usually very peaceful. Every gorilla seems to know its place in the order of things, and very little fighting takes place. The troop spends its days slowly wandering from place to place, eating as it goes. In many ways, gorillas seem to have the kind of simple life that some people say they would like to have.

At the end of every day, gorillas build nests to sleep in. They may build them on the ground or up in trees, and they use whatever materials happen to be handy.

The silverback is the strongest male in a gorilla group. It is his responsibility to protect the other members of the group, if the need arises. For this reason, silverbacks are more aggressive than other gorillas, and more "touchy." A silverback can get very angry very fast.

Every gorilla has its place in the troop. The "boss" is the oldest male silverback. He may have several assistants, called blackbacks.

SILVERBACK

FEMALE WITH YOUNG

Females with babies have more status than females that don't have them. There are usually twice as many females in a troop as males.

BLACKBACK

FEMALE WITHOUT YOUNG

When a gorilla troop moves from place to place, the silverback usually takes the lead, followed by the other males, and then by the females. Wherever the leading silverback wants to go, the other members of the troop will go, too.

① ② ③ ④

Like people, gorillas use sounds and facial expressions to let others know what they are thinking and feeling. Here are some of the expressions that gorillas use. Can you tell what they are expressing?

1-Anger, 2-Happiness, 3-Aggression, 4-Anxiety

In general, gorillas in a troop treat each other with kindness and consideration. Even the powerful silverback may show gentleness and patience with the young.

The main activity of a gorilla's day is eating. They get up rather early and spend most of the morning eating. During the hottest part of the day, they take time off for a nap. And then they keep eating until the sun goes down. During the course of a day, adult male gorillas can eat more than *40 pounds* (18 kilograms) of assorted leaves, stems, and roots from their favorite plants.

Gorillas really *love* to eat. As they chew, they often smack their lips together and grumble with contentment. Almost everything a gorilla eats comes from plants. Very rarely, they may eat a bird's egg or an insect. But 99-percent of their food is plants. To a gorilla, the dense forest is like a huge green restaurant.

As a rule, gorillas don't have to go very far to find food. They usually stay inside a rather small area called a *home range* (A) and find everything they need. At certain times of the year, however, special foods may ripen outside the home range. And the gorillas may travel some distance to get them (B). For example, Mountain gorillas may travel miles to get tender young bamboo shoots.

It is rare for gorillas to drink water in the wild. Most of the time, they get all the moisture they need from the plants they eat. Some of the juicier plants are almost half water.

Gorillas are fussy eaters. They know what they like, and that's all that they will usually eat. With some plants, they may eat only the leaves. With others, only the stalk or the roots. As the eat, they may carefully stack the parts they don't want in a neat pile.

Sometimes, the great strength of gorillas comes in handy when they are looking for food. It is an easy thing for an adult male gorilla to tear a banana tree to shreds, so he can get at the tender pith inside. But most of the time, gorillas need only a small part of their strength to get food.

WILD BANANA

WILD CELERY

GINGER

TAPIOCA

Different types of plants are available in different parts of Africa, so gorillas that live in different places have different diets. But they all eat a wide variety of plants. Mountain gorillas eat *more than 100* types of plants, including the ones shown here.

Most of the plant food that gorillas eat is coarse and tough. But their strong jaws have no trouble grinding it up.

GORILLA

① ②

HUMAN

It's easy to see why the jaws of a gorilla are so much more powerful than human jaws. The jaws are much larger, with bigger teeth. And they have huge muscles ① to close them. To see how the muscles close the jaws, feel the muscles on the side of your head ② as you chew.

Baby gorillas are tiny when they are born. On the average, they weigh only 4½ pounds (2 kilograms). If you consider that they may grow up to become 400-pound adults, you realize that they have a lot of growing to do! And they do start growing very fast.

Before long, they become very active. Adult gorillas tend to be slow-moving and reserved in their behavior. But young gorillas are just the opposite. They scamper around among the adults in search of as much fun as they can find. In general, the life of a young gorilla is a happy one, filled with all kinds of discoveries.

Like almost all baby animals, newborn gorillas are very easy to love. They have beautiful big dark eyes, and a sweet expression on their faces that is impossible to resist.

To help it hang on to its mother, a newborn gorilla has a very powerful grip. It can use both its hands and its feet to grab its mother's long hair.

Since a gorilla family is always on the move, baby gorillas must be able to move with their mothers almost as soon as they are born. When they are very young, they cling tightly to the hair on her stomach. When they get older, they ride on her back.

Gorilla babies and human babies develop in very similar ways during the first year of their lives. But the baby gorillas develop much *faster*. As you can see, they can do many things long before human babies. At the end of the year, however, the mental development of gorillas slows down—and the humans pass them by.

CRAWLING
9 Weeks

STANDING
20 Weeks

WALKING
34 Weeks

CRAWLING
37 Weeks

STANDING
43 Weeks

WALKING
52 Weeks

Like human children, young gorillas like to wrestle and tumble around a lot.

Older gorillas are too large and heavy to do much tree climbing. But the young gorillas do a lot of it.

An unusual game of young gorillas is the "conga line," when they form a chain and walk through the forest.

In the wild, gorilla mothers learn how to care for their babies by watching other mothers. In zoos, there may not be other mothers to watch. So zookeepers sometimes try to show new mothers what they should do.

Like human babies, young gorillas like to "wear" their food. This baby has made a fine hat out of a banana leaf.

Gorillas and people should be friends. After all, gorillas have many traits that we should admire. For one thing, they are generally peaceful animals. When they are left alone, they rarely bother anybody. And although they have tremendous strength, they rarely use it to hurt other creatures. There is a lot of evidence that gorillas are very intelligent...and they seem to live in an intelligent way.

Certainly, these are animals that we should learn to know better — and help to protect.

If you want to become friends with a gorilla, the best thing to do is act like a gorilla. Scientists who study gorillas have found that the animals will let them get very close if the scientists do things that gorillas do. If you ever meet a gorilla, here are a few things you should do.

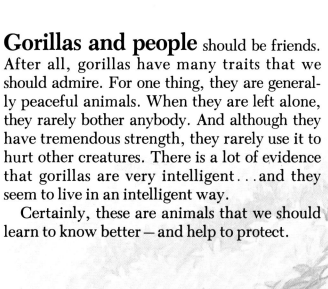

In the past, people took pride in killing gorillas. Hunters thought of gorillas as dangerous "big game" and tried to shoot as many as they could. Now that we know more about gorillas, the time has come to treat them in an entirely different way.

Most people have seen pictures of big gorillas beating their chests and charging —a frightening sight. But gorillas are not really violent animals. When they charge, they are simply trying to scare intruders away.

If a silverback is successful in scaring an intruder away, he doesn't follow after them and try to hurt them. Instead, he turns and walks peacefully off into the forest.

Stay down. And be quiet. A gorilla that stands up and gets noisy is usually angry. And if you do these things, gorillas will think that you are angry.

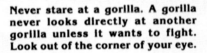

Never stare at a gorilla. A gorilla never looks directly at another gorilla unless it wants to fight. Look out of the corner of your eye.

Eat a leaf. To gorillas, this is a very peaceful gesture. Gorillas that eat together are usually friendly.

Scientists who have been studying Mountain gorillas have shown the gorillas that people are not always violent and destructive. As a result, certain groups of gorillas will let people get very close to them. They seem to want to get to know us, too.

In zoos, gorillas and people have been looking at each other for many years. When you look at these pictures of gorillas that were taken in zoos (above and below), it's clear that the gorillas find us just as interesting—and perhaps as amusing—as we sometimes find them.

The future of gorillas is linked to the survival of the forests in which they live. All three subspecies can only find the food they need in dense forests, so they will surely die out if all the forests are cut down.

Unfortunately, this is just what is happening in many parts of Africa. People are cutting down the trees at an alarming rate, to make room for farms and to sell the lumber. There is a need for more farmland because the human population of Africa is growing very fast. Every year, there are more people, and more food must be produced to feed them.

In some places, the trees are left standing, but cattle are brought in to eat the plants that gorillas normally eat — so there is not enough left for the gorillas. In other places, people actually hunt gorillas for food. It is against the law to kill gorillas, but hungry people often ignore the law.

The most endangered of the gorillas are the Mountain gorillas. The entire population of these magnificent animals is found in only a few small forests. And there are large populations of hungry people nearby. Twenty years ago, there were probably more than 15,000 Mountain gorillas. But today, there are probably fewer than 500. Clearly, unless something is done *now* to preserve their forests and protect them from hunters, the Mountain gorillas will be gone in just a few years.

Western Lowland and Eastern Lowland gorillas are a little better off. There are more of them, and their ranges are much larger. But the desstruction of the forests will eventually bring them to the brink of extinction as well, if it isn't stopped.

If we cannot save the natural habitats of gorillas in Africa, there may be another way to save at least *some* gorillas. Over the past 25 years, many zoos have learned how to breed and raise Western Lowland gorillas. If they are given a chance, they would probably be able to raise Eastern Lowland and Mountain gorillas as well.

As you have seen in this book, gorillas are really peaceful creatures that like to mind their own business. All they ask of humans is that we leave them alone and leave them a place to live. If we can find some way to do this, they are perfectly capable of surviving, as they have survived for millions of years.